ANTONIO VIV~~

L'E
SU.
DER S ...MER
L'ÉTÉ

Concerto for Violin, Strings and Basso continuo
G minor/g-Moll/Sol mineur
Op. 8/2
(RV 315)
Edited by/Herausgegeben von/Édition
Simon Launchbury

Ernst Eulenburg Ltd
London · Mainz · New York · Paris · Tokyo · Zürich

CONTENTS/INHALT/CONTENU

Performing material based on this edition is available from the publisher/
Der hier veröffentlichte Notentext ist auch als Aufführungsmaterial beim Verlag erhältlich/
Le matériel d'exécution réalisé à partir de cette édition est disponible chez l'éditeur

Ernst Eulenburg Ltd
48 Great Marlborough Street
London W1V 2BN

PREFACE

The *Four Seasons* are the first four of twelve concertos published as the *opera ottava* of Vivaldi by Le Cene of Amsterdam c.1725 with the title: 'Il Cimento dell' Armonia e dell' Invenzione' ('The Contest of Harmony and Invention'). Vivaldi added titles to several of his works, as was fashionable at the time, but the *Four Seasons* are unique in that they are prefaced by descriptive sonnets, assumed to be by the composer himself, which, as he writes in the dedicatory epistle, '[. . .] explain the music more easily'. The sections of the sonnets were initialled and the phrases inserted in the instrumental parts at the appropriate place. As well as the sonnets themselves, Vivaldi also added narrative captions to certain passages to highlight the descriptive nature of the music. This text matter is set out in a conflicting and generally haphazard manner in the source and a certain amount of tacit editorial adjustment has been made in the present edition particularly concerning the consistency of spelling and capitalization.

As there is no extant autograph the present edition is based on a copy of the early edition by Le Cene, now in the British Library, London (detailed in the Textual Notes below). This source contains many phrasing and dynamic markings, and any editorial additions are for the sake of conformity between identical sections and unanimity between the parts; these are indicated within square brackets or in the case of slurs and ties as broken ligatures. The notational distinction of the two forms of staccato marking found in the source (i.e., the stroke and the dot) has been retained in this edition. Where a tempo indication appears with a dynamic mark in the source, e.g., *p e larghetto*, the tempo mark is placed above the system and the dynamic marking below in this edition.

The term *Organo* in the instrumental bass section is taken to mean an appropriate keyboard instrument, most certainly a harpsichord in the present context. The indication *Tasto solo* (without harmonization) is only occasionally terminated with a *Tutti* marking in the source; other necessary *Tutti* markings have been supplied editorially.

The Italian commentary – based on the prefatory sonnets – contains some minor inconsistencies of spelling, capitalization, punctuation, etc., in the sources. These texts have not been modernized in this edition neither have they been detailed in the Textual Notes.

Simon Launchbury

VORWORT

Die *Vier Jahreszeiten* sind die ersten der zwölf als op. 8 (*opera ottava*) erschienenen Konzerte von Vivaldi, die um 1725 von Le Cene in Amsterdam unter dem Titel *Il Cimento dell'Armonia e dell' Invenzione* („Der Wettstreit zwischen Harmonie und Einfall") herausgegeben wurden. Der damaligen Mode entsprechend hat Vivaldi mehreren seiner Werke einen Titel gegeben; die *Vier Jahreszeiten* sind jedoch insofern einzigartig, als ihnen Sonette vorangestellt sind, die vermutlich vom Komponisten selbst stammen und über die er in seinem Widmungsschreiben äußert, sie „sollten die Musik verständlicher machen". Den einzelnen Abschnitten der Sonette sind Großbuchstaben vorangestellt, und die Worte der Sonette stehen in den Stimmen an entsprechender Stelle. Vivaldi hat neben den Sonetten zudem beschreibende Überschriften für bestimmte Passagen eingefügt, um den deskriptiven Charakter der Musik herauszustellen. Dieser Aspekt des Textanteils in den *Vier Jahreszeiten* stellt sich in der Quelle (also der Erstausgabe) auf widersprüchliche und durchweg zufällige Art und Weise dar; so hat der Herausgeber dieser Ausgabe prinzipiell bestimmte Berichtigungen besonders im Hinblick auf Übereinstimmung von Wortlaut und den erwähnten Großbuchstaben stillschweigend vorgenommen.

Das Autograph ist nicht erhalten; deshalb beruht diese Ausgabe auf einem Exemplar der Erstausgabe von Le Cene. Es ist heute im Besitz der British Library, London, und wird in den Einzelanmerkungen näher beschrieben. Diese Quelle enthält viele Eintragungen für Phrasierungen und Dynamik. Herausgeberzusätze stellen die Übereinstimmung identischer Stellen und der Stimmen untereinander sicher. Man erkennt sie an eckigen Klammern oder gestrichelten Phrasierungs- oder Legato-

bögen. Keil und Punkt als *staccato*-Vorschrift sind in dieser Ausgabe gemäß der Quelle beibehalten. Bei Tempo-Angaben mit dem Zusatz einer dynamischen Vorschrift, beispielsweise *p e larghetto*, steht in dieser Ausgabe die Vorschrift für das Tempo über dem System, für die Dynamik darunter.

Mit *Organo* in der Baßgruppe ist ein geeignetes Tasteninstrument gemeint, hier mit großer Wahrscheinlichkeit ein Cembalo. Am Ende einer *Tasto solo*-Passage (also ohne Harmonisierung) steht in der Quelle nicht immer *Tutti*. Diese und weitere *Tutti*-Vorschriften hat der Herausgeber hinzugesetzt.

Der italienische Kommentar auf der Grundlage der vorangestellten Sonette enthält in den Quellen einige unbedeutende Widersprüche in Schreibweise, Großschreibung, Zeichensetzung usw. In dieser Ausgabe wurden weder diese Texte modernisiert noch in den Einzelanmerkungen näher erläutert.

Simon Launchbury
Übersetzung Norbert Henning

PRÉFACE

Les *Quatre saisons* sont les quatre premiers de douze concertos publiés comme *opera ottava* de Vivaldi par Le Cene, à Amsterdam, vers 1725, sous le titre de «Il Cimento dell'Armonia e dell'Invenzione» («Le combat de l'Harmonie et de l'Invention»). Selon l'usage en faveur à son époque, Vivaldi ajouta des titres à plusieurs de ses œuvres mais les *Quatres saisons* représentent un cas exceptionnel à cet égard car elles sont précédées de sonnets descriptifs, sans doute écrits par le compositeur lui-même, qui, ainsi qu'il le précise dans sa dédicace, «[. . .] expliquent plus facilement la musique.» Aux différentes sections des sonnets furent attribuées des lettres et les vers furent insérés dans la partition aux endroits correspondants. En plus des sonnets, Vivaldi illustra quelques passages de légendes narratives qui soulignent la nature descriptive de ces concertos. Ces textes sont généralement placés de façon indécise et fortuite dans la source. Un certain nombre de corrections tacites ont donc été effectuées dans cette édition, notamment en ce qui concerne la cohérence de l'orthographe et des majuscules.

Comme il n'existe aucun manuscrit autographe des œuvres, notre édition s'appuie sur un exemplaire de la première édition de Le Cene conservé à la British Library de Londres (et analysé dans l'appareil critique ci-dessous). Cette source comporte de nombreuses indications de phrasé et de nuances dynamiques; les précisions éditoriales complémentaires ont pour objectif de rétablir la conformité entre sections identiques et la similarité des parties. Celles-ci sont placées entre crochets ou, dans le cas des liaisons et liaisons de phrasés, en pointillé. Les deux formes distinctes de notation du *staccato* figurant dans la source (tiret et point) ont été maintenues. Lorsque dans la source apparaît une indication de tempo accompagnée d'une nuance dynamique, par exemple *p e larghetto*, l'indication de tempo est placée au-dessus du système et l'indication dynamique en dessous.

Le terme *Organo* à la basse instrumentale désigne tout instrument à clavier approprié, et sûrement le clavecin dans ce contexte. La mention *Tasto solo* (sans harmonisation) n'est que rarement suivie de la notation de reprise du *Tutti* dans la source. Certaines indications de *Tutti* supplémentaires ont été rétablies à l'édition.

Le commentaire en italien – reposant sur les sonnets d'introduction – présente certaines incohérences mineures dans les sources quant à l'orthographe, les majuscules, la ponctuation, etc. Ces textes n'ont pas été modernisés pour cette édition, ni ne font l'objet d'une analyse dans l'appareil critique.

Simon Launchbury
Traduction Agnès Ausseur

2

Sonetto Dimostrativo
Sopra il Concerto Intitolato

L'ESTADE

DEL SIG.^{re} D. ANTONIO VIVALDI

A Sotto dura Staggion dal Sole accesa
  Langue L'huom, langue 'l gregge, ed arde il Pino;
B Scioglie il Cucco la Voce, e tosto intesa
C Canta la Tortorella e 'l gardelino.

D Zeffiro dolce Spira, mà contesa
  Muove Borea improviso al Suo vicino;
E E piange il Pastorel, perche Sospesa
  Teme fiera borasca, e 'l Suo destino:

F Toglie alle membra lasse il Suo riposo
  Il timore de' Lampi, e tuoni fieri
  E de mosche, e mosponi il Stuol furioso! /e

G Ah che pur troppo i Suoi timor Son veri
  Tuona e fulmina il Ciel e grandinoso
  Tronca il capo alle Spiche e a'grani alteri

Sonnet/Sonett/Sonnet

SUMMER

A Under the harsh weather set ablaze by the sun
   man and beast languish, and the pine tree is parched.
B The cuckoo loosens his voice, and soon
C the turtle dove and the goldfinch join him in song.

D Sweet Zephyr blows, but in challenge
   Boreas suddenly moves to his side,
E and the shepherd boy cries because he is afraid
   of the fierce impending storm, and his fate.

F Rest is denied his weary limbs
   by the fear of lightning and violent thunder
   and the furious swarm of flies and bluebottles.

G Ah, but sadly his fears are real;
   the sky thunders and flashes, and with hail
   cuts off the head of corn stalks and of lofty wheat.

Translation Peter Owens

SOMMER

A In der sengenden Glut der Sonne ermatten Mensch und Tier,
   und die Pinien verdorren.
B Der Kuckuck erhebt seine Stimme, und bald schon
C fallen Taube und Stieglitz in seinen Gesang mit ein.

D Sacht' weht der Zephir, doch plötzlich stellt sich ihm
   herausfordernd der Nordwind zur Seite.
E Der Hirtenjunge schreit auf, voller Angst vor dem
   drohenden unbändigen Sturm und vor seinem Schicksal.

F Verwehrt ist seinen müden Gliedern die Ruhe
   aus Angst vor Blitz und krachendem Donner
   und den wilden Schwärmen von Fliegen und Brummern.

G Ach, seine Befürchtungen sind nur allzu wahr;
   vom Himmel ertönt Donner, leuchten Blitze,
   und Hagelschauer verwüsten die wogenden Getreidefelder.

Übersetzung Esther Dubielzig

L'ÉTÉ

A Pendant les jours torrides enflammés de soleil
   l'homme et la bête reposent et le pin se dessèche.
B Le coucou élève la voix et bientôt
C la tourterelle et le chardonneret se joignent à lui.

D Le doux Zéphyr souffle mais, le défiant,
   Boréas soudain l'accompagne,
E et le berger pleure de peur
   face à l'orage terrible qui menace et face à son destin.

F Point de repos pour ses membres fatigués
   devant la crainte de l'éclair et du violent tonnerre,
   et de la nuée furieuse des mouches.

G Ah! Que sa crainte est juste,
   le ciel gronde et s'embrase et la grêle
   tranche les épis de maïs.

Traduction Agnès Ausseur

IE = First edition, undated c. 1725, in sets of parts, title-page:
IL CIMENTO DELL' ARMONIA/E DELL' IN-
VENTIONE/CONCERTI/a 4 e 5/[. . .]/DA
D. ANTONIO VIVALDI/[. . .]/OPERA OTTAVA/
Libro Primo/A AMSTERDAM/spesà di MICHELE
CARLO LE CENE/Librario/No. 520
Set consulted: British Library, London,
GB-Lbm g.33.c.

n(n) = note(s)
b(b) = bar(s)

Concerto No. 2

Mov. I

25 B.c. IE reads:

49 Vl. II n1 *f* in IE

57 B.c. IE reads:

110 Vla. n1 c in IE

113, 114 Vl. pr. nn1–3 slurred in IE

168 B.c. n2 lacks sharp in IE

Mov. II

19 Vl. II n10 C♯′ in IE

Mov. III

16 Vl. pr. n7 hand-written ✕ (= sharp) in IE

113 Vl. I/II n7 ♭ in IE

Simon Launchbury

CONCERTO No. 2 L'ESTATE

Antonio Vivaldi
(1678–1741)
Op. 8/2
RV 315

I. **Allegro non molto**

LANGUIDEZZA PER IL CALDO

A Sotto dura staggion dal sole accesa langue l'huom, langue'l gregge, ed

Violino principale

Violino I

Violino II

Viola

Organo e Violoncello [Basso continuo]

arde il pino;

Vl. pr.

I — Vl.

II

Vla.

B. c.

Edited by Simon Launchbury
© 1982 Ernst Eulenburg Ltd
Revised edition © 1996 Ernst Eulenburg Ltd
and Ernst Eulenburg & Co GmbH

No. 1221   EE 7037

ZEFFIRETTI DOLCI
D Zeffiro dolce spira,

EE 7037

IL PIANTO DEL VILLANELLO
E e piange il pastorel, perche sospesa teme fiera borasca, e'l suo destino;

EE 7037

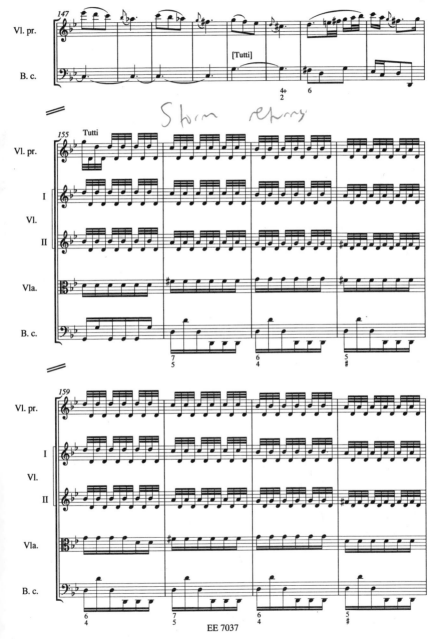

EE 7037

10

12

13

EE 7037

14

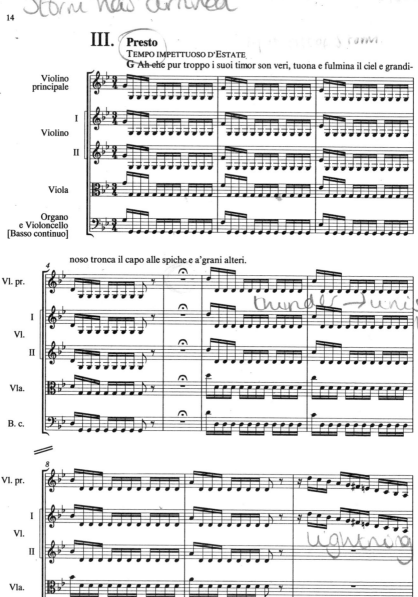

III. Presto
TEMPO IMPETTUOSO D'ESTATE
G Ah che pur troppo i suoi timor son veri, tuona e fulmina il ciel e grandi-

noso tronca il capo alle spiche e a'grani alteri.

EE 7037

EE 7037

★) = sul D, G

20

EE 7037